Finding

BIBLICAL FELLOWSHIP

FOR WHERE TWO OR THREE ARE GATHERED
TOGETHER IN MY NAME, THERE AM I IN THE
MIDST OF THEM. –MATTHEW 18:20

David
KERCHER

Pete
SALAS

BEND • OREGON

www.thebereancall.org

FINDING BIBLICAL FELLOWSHIP
David Kercher & Pete Salas

Finding
BIBLICAL
FELLOWSHIP

†

FOR WHERE TWO OR THREE ARE GATHERED TOGETHER IN MY NAME, THERE AM I IN THE MIDST OF THEM. –MATTHEW 18:20

David KERCHER

Pete SALAS

CONTENTS

PREFACE

Over the past two-plus decades, the most common request that is received by the Berean Call staff is, "Can you help us find a good, solid church in our area?" Over the years, Dave Hunt and T.A. McMahon have written material in an effort to help believers look for and find a church fellowship to which they can commit themselves to and begin to use their gifts to minister to the saints. That, however, is getting increasingly difficult. More and more churches have become caught up in doctrinal error to the extent that the saints simply cannot commit themselves to such leadership and teachings (2 Tim. 4:3-4). That being said, this booklet is not intended to encourage those who are simply unwilling to submit to any church authority or who are given to divisiveness. Our prayer is that this booklet will encourage you to "find biblical fellowship" that is operating according to the Scriptures rather than what has, for the most part, become the traditions of men.

PART ONE

The AMAZING POWER OF THE LIFE OF CHRIST IN HIS CHURCH

DAVID KERCHER

INTRODUCTION

In the following chapters, I would like to focus on some basic truths about the church and the life of Christ at work in His church, in and through His disciples, as they minister to one another using the gifts that He has given to them for that purpose.

My goal is to help believers to understand and be encouraged to believe that Christ is pleased to work with even a very small group of believers who start off meeting in a home or other convenient meeting place, reading the scriptures together, praying together, breaking bread together, and expecting God to provide all that is necessary for the edification of the assembled group by the Holy Spirit working through the Word and through each other for the edification of the whole.

I would also like to encourage believers to reckon that this is not an oddity but rather a very much-approved beginning for an assembly: "For where two or three are gathered together in my name, there am I in the midst of them" (Matt. 18:20).

Sometimes believers may be hesitant to consider beginning a fellowship in their home with just a few other like-minded believers because they think to themselves, "Where are we going to find a pastor? Who is going to preach the sermon? Who is going to teach? Where will we find a worship team?" My prayer is that when you have finished prayerfully reading this series of articles, you may begin to consider the possibility that you do not need a seminary-trained pastor or a worship team, but rather that you will realize that you do not need either.

Chapter One

HIS STRENGTH IS MADE PERFECT IN WEAKNESS

. . . and God hath chosen the weak things of the world to confound the things which are mighty.
(1 Cor. 1:27)

. . . for my strength is made perfect in weakness. (2 Cor. 12:9)

In this first chapter, I would like to have us look at some scriptural examples of how our Lord chooses His servants and what qualifications He demands.

All through the scripture God has shown us in example after example that He does not choose His servants based on their strength, knowledge, speaking ability, physical stature, or any other natural prowess; but rather He chooses His servants in their weakness in order that His power may be demonstrated. What He needs are men who will trust Him, in spite of their weakness, to fulfill His Word through them.

ABRAHAM

Now the LORD had said unto Abram, Get thee out of thy country, and from thy kindred, and from thy father's house, unto a land that I will shew thee: And I will make of thee a great nation, and I will bless thee, and make thy name great; and thou shalt be a blessing: And I will bless them that bless thee, and curse him that curseth thee: and in thee shall all families of the earth be blessed. So Abram departed, as the LORD had spoken unto him; and Lot went with him: and Abram was seventy and five years old when he departed out of Haran. And Abram took Sarai his wife, and Lot his brother's son, and all their substance that they had gathered, and the souls that they had gotten in Haran; and they went forth to go into the land of Canaan; and into the land of Canaan they came. (Gen. 12:1-5)

I would like us to take note here that Abraham (at this time still called *Abram*) was 75 years old when the Lord came to him and told him to leave his home country and people, his kindred, and his father's house and become a sojourner, traveling to a land that he did not know. I believe that this was very difficult for Abraham. He was not a young man, full of vigor and desire for adventure, but he was an elderly man, whom I believe would have much rather stayed home among his family and people. This may have seemed a very fearful prospect to Abraham, but he did it anyway because he believed God!

> *By faith Abraham, when he was called to go out into a place which he should after receive for an inheritance, obeyed; and he went out, not knowing whither he went. By faith he sojourned in the land of promise, as in a strange country, dwelling in tabernacles with Isaac and Jacob, the heirs with him of the same promise. . . . (Heb. 11:8-9)*

Abraham was not chosen because of his great strength of character or his great courage. We see this recorded for us in Genesis 20. When Abraham was faced with a situation that he considered dangerous to himself because of Sarah's physical beauty, he lied to save himself, even though it put his wife in a precarious situation.

> *And Abraham journeyed from thence toward the south country, and dwelled between Kadesh and Shur, and sojourned in Gerar. And Abraham said of Sarah his wife, She is my sister: and Abimelech king of Gerar sent, and took Sarah (Gen. 20:1-2).*

[I recommend that you read all of Genesis chapter 20.]

There are many aspects to this story that could be looked at and are enlightening concerning God's care for and protection of His servant who has placed his trust in Him. However, the one aspect I would like us to look at now is that I believe at least one reason that God was faithful to record this episode in Abraham's life was so that we could consider the fact that *Abraham had weakness even as we do.* In fact, this is quite a shocking example of cowardice. (Please understand that I am not trying to pick on Abraham. Abraham is one of my heroes of the faith. There are other examples in the scriptures that we could look at that show great courage of faith on this man's part.) Abraham's great strength was not in himself and who he was as a man, but rather it was in the fact that he was *willing to believe God.* He was willing to step out in faith, trusting what God had said to him, trusting that God would be faithful to His Word—even though he had no idea how God was going to accomplish it.

MOSES

When God appeared to Moses in the burning bush after Moses had failed to be the deliverer of Israel that he thought he was supposed to be, and running from Pharaoh, then ending up spending the next 40 years tending sheep in the desert, Moses was thoroughly convinced that he was incapable of speaking for Israel. He was content to let his brother, Aaron, who apparently had some speaking ability, speak for him. God, in His great patience and kindness, allowed Moses to learn by experience that *he* could—and should—be the one to speak for Israel in obedience to God's command. (Consider how quickly Aaron stumbled when Moses left him to look after Israel while Moses went up the mountain to receive the commandments!)

GIDEON

The Lord had to pare down Gideon's army to 300 men (a ridiculously small number) that He would use to go against (and defeat) an army of Midianites and Amalekites, whose number was so large that even their camels were described as "without number, as the sand by the seashore."

> *And the Midianites and the Amalekites and all the children of the east lay along in the valley like grasshoppers for multitude; and their camels were without number, as the sand by the sea side for multitude. (Judg. 7:12)*

DAVID

Samuel was ready to conclude that Eliab, David's brother, was the Lord's choice for king of Israel because of his stature:

But the LORD said unto Samuel, Look not on his
countenance, or on the height of his stature;
because I have refused him: for the LORD seeth
not as man seeth; for man looketh on the
outward appearance, but the LORD looketh on
the heart. (1 Sam. 16:7)

PAUL

The apostle Paul, who taught us the most on this subject, learned these things through hard experience. Even though the Lord's ministry through Paul was vast and powerful, there is strong evidence that Paul had to conduct his ministry in spite of much personal weakness and infirmity. He had to endure the following criticism from those whom he referred to as false apostles in 2 Corinthians:

For his letters, say they, are weighty and
powerful; but his bodily presence is weak, and
his speech contemptible. (2 Cor. 10:10)

Since this criticism was made by those to whom Paul referred as false apostles and, therefore, unbelievers, we cannot consider them to be good judges and so must be careful not to give too much credence to what they have to say about Paul, except that we can, at least, conclude that Paul's physical presence and speaking did not impress them. Later, in chapter 11 of 2 Corinthians, Paul referred to himself:

But though I be rude in speech, yet not in
knowledge.... (2 Cor. 11:6)

Paul may have been mocking the false apostles when he referred to himself as "rude in speech," but perhaps not. Knowing how the Lord works, I think it is quite likely that Paul did struggle with some significant physical disadvantages that he had to trust the Lord to work through in order to accomplish his ministry. He expressed this in 2 Corinthians 12:

And he said unto me, My grace is sufficient
for thee: for my strength is made perfect in
weakness. Most gladly therefore will I rather
glory in my infirmities, that the power of Christ
may rest upon me. Therefore I take pleasure
in infirmities, in reproaches, in necessities, in
persecutions, in distresses for Christ's sake:
for when I am weak, then am I strong. (2 Cor.
12:9-10)

OTHERS

There are many more examples in scripture that we could look at and much more that could be said on this, but the point that I would really like to stress here is that this truth is not just for the men who are examples for us in scripture or possibly some church leaders whom we may know.

Moreover, this truth concerning God's purpose and willingness to gift believers for ministry in His church who are weak in themselves and do not see themselves as capable, according to their natural judgment of their own abilities, is foundational and essential truth that applies to all of God's family of believers.

We must not make the mistake of basing our decision on whether or not to step out in obedience to God on our own natural assessment of our abilities.

It is *Christ's* life and power that He is working out through us, through believers, through His Church, through His bride; and He often uses the most unlikely vessels to accomplish His task. We must reckon this to be true for each of us, in the face of our own weakness, and determine to trust *Him* rather than ourselves. We must also be ready to stand against the enemy of our souls who will try to use our own infirmities against us to accuse us and tempt us to become discouraged and give up. The more effective the life of Christ is being lived through us by faith, the fiercer shall be this warfare.

> *Finally, my brethren, be strong in the Lord, and in the power of his might. Put on the whole armour of God, that ye may be able to stand against the wiles of the devil. (Eph. 6:10-11)*

The truths that I have brought forth in this chapter are intended to be presented as foundational understanding for the following chapters, offered as instruction for the saints on the amazing power of the life of Christ being worked out in His church.

Chapter Two

"IT IS GOD WHICH WORKETH IN YOU BOTH TO WILL AND TO DO OF HIS GOOD PLEASURE"

—*Philippians 2:13*

In this chapter we will be looking at the purpose and ultimate goal of the gifts that have been given by Jesus Christ to each member of the body of Christ (every believer). We will, of course, be desirous of knowing what is the specific identity of our gift; but it is important for us to realize that, for most of us (with perhaps some exceptions) the discovery of the identity of our gift will not come by vision or special revelation but will most likely come through trusting and obeying.

It is not likely that we'll be able to accurately discern the identity of our gift by examining our feelings. One of the most basic lessons that we must learn as believers is that we cannot let ourselves be led by our feelings. Our feelings (emotions) will nearly always lead us astray if we allow ourselves to be led by them. We must be led by *faith*, which is sometimes in direct opposition to our feelings. I believe the most certain path for us when it comes to discerning our gift is first of all to believe that Christ *has* gifted us for service to the body of Christ, and then committing ourselves to Him in prayer for this service, being obedient to whatever simple task He puts before us, cheerfully obeying and trusting Him to direct our steps. We know that *". . . we are his workmanship, created in Christ Jesus unto good works, which God hath before ordained that we should walk in them"* (Eph. 2:10).

We may consider what we believe are our strengths and offer ourselves to Him, all the while recognizing that any supernatural gifting that may be ultimately revealed in and through us might not turn out to be associated at all with what we perceive as our strengths! However, just as the waters of the Jordan did not begin to part until the priests' feet touched the water, so we will likely not begin to really understand what our gift is until we step forward in obedience. *For it is God which worketh in you both to will and to do of his good pleasure* (Php. 2:13). Count on God to fulfill this scripture in you. Pay attention to the leanings that He gives you as you love the saints with an "unfeigned" love.

It is also important for us to realize that the grace that Christ gives us in the exercising of our gift allows us to grow in the ministering of the gift as we grow in Christ and as we continue to give what we have been given. Our Lord does not expect us to be instantly skillful or mature in our ministry but is very gracious in our feeble beginnings; and He provides the power and effectiveness of our ministry not based on our strength but rather on His strength. As we faithfully continue to minister the gift to the body of Christ in our weakness, we will grow in confidence as we see His faithfulness and strength working through us; we will likely begin to see that we are becoming increasingly comfortable/skillful in our ministering of the gift!

If you are a believer in Christ Jesus, you *have been* gifted in some way, supernaturally, by the Lord Jesus Christ, specifically for the purpose of edifying or serving the body of Christ (the church).

> *But unto every one of us is given grace according*
> *to the measure of the gift of Christ (Eph. 4:7).*

Notice, first of all, that there are two things spoken of here: *the gift,* which is given by Christ in a particular measure to the believer, and *the grace*, which is given, that is sufficient for the accomplishing of that gift (ministry). Notice also, that the gift is given *"unto every one of us."* Every believer has been gifted, and every believer has been given *"grace according to the measure of the gift."* Each of us has been given a gift (or gifts), measured out precisely by Christ, and exactly appropriate for the way in which He intends to use us in *His* ministry to the body of Christ. It is very important that we, as part of this body, reckon this to be true for us and embrace this truth, actively looking for God's leading in the fulfillment of it.

This scripture also reveals to us that a measure of grace has been given to each of us, which is exactly sufficient to enable us to accomplish the ministering of that gift that we have received. The gift that He has given us is peculiar to *us*. It is not a general gift that is given in the same description and measure across the board to every believer but is a gift given by the wonderful wisdom of Christ and is exactly the way in which He desires to manifest Himself through that particular believer as the believer trusts Christ to do so and is obedient.

As we begin a discussion of the particular gifts listed and described in the scriptures (which are many), I want to stress that not all of the gifts must necessarily be present in a beginning assembly. Christ has given the authorization for beginning an assembly with as little as two or three saints. *For where two or three are gathered together in my name, there am I in the midst of them* (Mat. 18:20).

Where Christ is, everything that is important is there; and where two or three are gathered in His name, trusting Him, all that is needed will be provided.

Consider the way the church was first being established throughout Europe in Acts. Paul and Barnabas (and later Silas) would go to a city and lead several to Christ. They would then begin to disciple that group of believers until they could be left to function as a fellowship on their own. Paul and Barnabas/Silas would then leave them for a while, go on, and do the same elsewhere. Eventually they would return when the brethren had matured sufficiently to the degree that there were men who would qualify as elders, and would then appoint those elders. Thus the church they would continue to grow.

Remember, the church is a very powerful *living organism*. Nothing can stop it (except perhaps unbelief and disobedience, and the error that always follows that scenario).

I think of examples in God's creation that might illustrate this truth. Think of the starfish. It has been said that if a starfish is cut into pieces, as long as there is a part of the central portion of the body (the heart) in each piece, then each piece will grow into a new starfish. When a group of two or more saints meet together, believing God's word concerning the gifts they have been given, trusting Him to work in and through them for each other and the whole, and being obedient, God will provide what is necessary for the growth and functioning of the body.

So what are these gifts, and what is their purpose? Let's look first at the list that is given in Ephesians 4. There are more

gifts than the ones listed here, and we will look at some of
the others later; but let's start with these five:

> *And he gave some, apostles; and some, prophets;*
> *and some, evangelists; and some, pastors and*
> *teachers; For the perfecting of the saints, for the*
> *work of the ministry, for the edifying of the body*
> *of Christ. . . . (Eph. 4:11-12)*

Notice that there are five gifts listed here, and their purpose
is clearly given. Before we try to identify and understand
their individual functions in the church, I would like us to
look at and understand their purpose and the ultimate *goal*
of their functions, which will then make it easier to discern
their functions. This will also, I believe, make it easier for
us to get our sights aimed properly as we begin to work out
the ministering of our own gift for the blessing of the body.
The gifts are for:

1. "The perfecting of the saints"

"The perfecting of the saints" is the process of ministering
to the saints toward and with the goal of maturity in Christ.
The word "perfecting" sees application when the saints are
equipped and enabled to walk in obedience to God's word,
walking in His wisdom, and seeing effectiveness in their
ministries.

2. "For the work of ministry"

There are all kinds of ministry to the body of Christ for the purpose of edifying the saints and bringing them to maturity.

3. "For the edifying of the body of Christ"

In other words, for the building up or strengthening the saints, making them more prepared to walk in the Spirit, to take God at His word, to discern the good and perfect will of God for their daily lives, to wear the armor of God, to encourage them in the exercise and development of their gifts/ministries in the body, etc.

Let's now look at the ultimate goal of the gifts:

> Till we all come in the unity of the faith, and of the knowledge of the Son of God, unto a perfect man, unto the measure of the stature of the fulness of Christ. . . . (Eph. 4:13)

The ultimate goal is that *we would come to full maturity in Christ*, but we must all come:

1. In the unity of the faith

> There is one body, and one Spirit, even as ye are called in one hope of your calling; One Lord, one faith, one baptism, One God and Father of all,

who is above all, and through all, and in you all.
(Eph. 4:4-6)

We will never come to maturity in Christ if we are not fully
convinced of the truths spoken in Eph. 4:4-6, nor will we be
effective in ministry to the body of Christ.

2. In the knowledge of the Son of God

That I may know him, and the power of his
resurrection, and the fellowship of his sufferings,
being made conformable unto his death. . . .
(Php. 3:10)

We will never come to maturity in Christ without *knowing*
Christ.

One of the fruits of the body that has grown up by means of
the ministry of these gifts, working together according to
the measure and wisdom of the Lord, is soundness in doctrine and the ability to recognize what is false.

That we henceforth be no more children, tossed
to and fro, and carried about with every wind
of doctrine, by the sleight of men, and cunning
craftiness, whereby they lie in wait to deceive; But
speaking the truth in love, may grow up into him
in all things, which is the head, even Christ. . . .
(Eph. 4:14-15)

When the body of Christ is allowed to grow up with all of its parts functioning, using their gifts in accordance with the measure of both the gift and the associated grace that has been given to minister the gift, the body can grow in a healthy way. There are many safeguards given for the body.

One of the benefits of a healthy functioning body is soundness in doctrine. Consider the human body. When our physical body is healthy, there are systems that have been placed in the body by the Lord that are designed to fight off disease, germs, illness, etc.; but when the body is not functioning in a healthy way, these defense systems do not function as well, and we get sick. The same is true with the body of Christ. When we disregard the teaching of the scripture concerning the functioning of the body ministry and substitute man's ideas for body ministry instead, we leave unused some of the safeguards that the Lord has established for the church; and we leave the church vulnerable to attack.

I believe that this is a major contributor to the mass exodus into error that we see today in the church overall and that has been going on for many years. I believe that we are in the time of the falling away, and it is critical now for the church to return to simple obedience to the scriptures in regard to the body ministry of the church in order that we may grow to maturity and weather the storm.

Let us now look at the description of a healthy functioning body given in the following verse:

> *From whom the whole body fitly joined together and compacted by that which every joint supplieth, according to the effectual working in the measure of every part, maketh increase of the body unto the edifying of itself in love. (Eph. 4:16)*

Let's break this down, because there are so many things to be learned from these verses about the healthy and powerful function of the body.

1. From whom

Whom refers to Christ, who is the head of the church as seen from the previous verse. Christ is the head of the church overall as well as the head of the local assembly. It is imperative that our attention be on Him, individually and as an assembly. We worship Him, study Him, trust and obey Him, allow Him to empower our ministries one to another, and expect Him to manifest Himself in each of us and through each of us for one another and for the lost.

2. The whole body fitly joined together

Fitly joined is a fine woodworker's or wooden shipbuilder's terminology. It comes from the art of wood joinery. Think of a fine woodworking joint, like a dovetail joint, finger joint, or a mortise and tenon joint. We are being assembled together. *"In whom ye also are builded together for an habitation of God through the Spirit"* (Eph. 2:22).

3. And compacted by that which every joint supplieth

When the joint is prepared correctly (fitly), it will have to be driven together (compacted). This scripture is teaching us that the necessary compacting is being done by *that ministry that every part of the body is supplying.* It is not going to be done successfully by one member, whom we may call a pastor and whom we have designated to be the sole "compactor." That comes from man's wisdom. It is not according to the revelation of scripture and is a great mistake. Our refusal to hear God's word concerning the function of the gifts in the body and the way in which Christ is building His church is in great measure the cause of the amazing amount of error and failure that has manifested itself in the professing church overall.

4. According to the effectual working

Here is an amazing truth to grasp. God is revealing to us that the supernatural gift that He has given to each member of the body *will be effective!* He is stating that when each member ministers his gift by faith, trusting Him for its effectiveness, *its working will be effective!* It will accomplish the result, which is the joining (assembling), the building up (edifying), of the body and all of the safeguards and blessings that go with it.

One of the evidences/validations of our gifting is this promised effectiveness. If we can be patient in attempting to identify our gift, we will likely begin to receive some feedback from the saints, indicating how they have been blessed by our ministry. This will usually come after much obedience and is a more certain indicator than our own introspection—especially if we *haven't* been obedient in ministering to the saints.

5. In the measure of every part

Again, Christ has measured out every gift precisely for its exact use in the body, through whom and for whom it will be used. He has pre-determined its effectiveness. It is not necessary that we get ourselves a hat or a shirt that has a title written on it: "I am a Teacher;" "I am a Prophet;" or "I am an Evangelist." Let us recognize that the blend of gifting is according to Christ's measure and is as unique to each individual believer as each individual believer is to the body of Christ.

6. Maketh increase of the body unto the edifying of itself

As each part does its work trusting Christ, the body will grow in strength and maturity and will edify itself.

7. In love

This is key to the function of the church and a healthy growth of the body. We must love one another with an unfeigned (genuine) love as we minister to the body.

Chapter Three

STEWARDS OF THE MANIFOLD GRACE OF GOD

As every man hath received the gift, even so minister the same one to another, as good stewards of the manifold grace of God. If any man speak, let him speak as the oracles of God; if any man minister, let him do it as of the ability which God giveth: that God in all things may be glorified through Jesus Christ, to whom be praise and dominion for ever and ever. Amen. (1 Pet. 4:10-11)

In chapter 1 we considered God's purposefulness in choosing weak vessels in order to show His strength and that we do well to consider this a reality for ourselves. In chapter 2 we considered the purpose and ultimate goal of the gifts that Christ has given to every believer. In this chapter, I would like us to consider the function of the individual gifts as they are ministered in, and for, the body of Christ. My intention in this article is not to try to give an in-depth and full teaching on the gifts but rather to give enough information to be helpful to those who believe that Christ has gifted believers for ministry to the body and would like some help in discerning what these ministries may look like when functioning in the body of Christ.

Let us consider the five gifts listed in Ephesians 4:

1. APOSTLE

When Peter addressed the other ten remaining apostles according to the record in Acts 1:15-26, he made it clear that they must choose a replacement for Judas from among those brethren who had been with them throughout the life and ministry of Jesus and who were witnesses of His resurrection. He also made it clear that the number of twelve apostles was a number that was necessary to keep intact for the apostolic ministry in order to fulfill scripture. I believe that this makes it clear that the original twelve apostles were a special group that had a special ministry, which will not be repeated. Then we see the Apostle Paul's calling, which is described in detail in Acts 9:3-18. Paul refers to himself later, in 1 Corinthians 15:8, as the last apostle that had seen the Lord after His resurrection and as "one born out of due time." So now we have the original twelve plus Paul, in his unique calling, who were witnesses of the Lord after His resurrection. As we know, Paul, Peter, John, and Matthew were also used to write scripture. This special privilege is unique and not to be repeated.

So now we might think: *"Now we have it: there's the original twelve plus Paul's unique calling and ministry to the Gentiles. That must be the sum of the apostles, and there will not be any more."* But then Paul throws a curve in it for us with his final greetings to the saints in Rome, where he says: *"Salute Andronicus and Junia, my kinsmen, and my fellow-prisoners, who are of note among the apostles, who also were in Christ before me"* (Rom. 16:7).

There are a lot of questions to be asked here: Who were Andronicus and Junia? These are Roman names, and they were apparently in Italy at the time. Paul referred to them not only as apostles but "of note among the apostles." Were they well known and highly regarded by the other apostles? Did they at some point share a prison cell with Paul? Were they in Christ before Paul, and he referred to them as his "kinsmen"? We have just not been given enough information from the scriptures to know very much about these brothers except what we can glean from this one verse. However, I believe that it is reasonable to conclude that they were not among those who traveled with Jesus during His earthly ministry and probably were not among those who were eyewitnesses of His resurrection; yet this passage appears to be identifying them as apostles. This seems to, at least, point to the possibility that there were others also who had been gifted with an apostolic ministry.

We know from Ephesians 4 that the gifts given were *"for the perfecting of the saints, for the work of the ministry, for the edifying of the body of Christ . . . "* (Eph. 4:12). The first gift on this list that Christ gave to the church is called *some apostles.* Was there only Paul and the original twelve apostles? Were Andronicus and Junia apostles also and then no more?

I believe the answer is given in the next three verses:

> *"Till we all come in the unity of the faith, and of the knowledge of the Son of God, unto a perfect man, unto the measure of the stature of the fulness of Christ: That we henceforth be no more children, tossed to and fro, and carried about with every wind of doctrine, by the sleight of men, and cunning craftiness, whereby they lie in wait to deceive; But speaking the truth in love, may grow up into him in all things, which is the head, even Christ . . . . "*
> *(Eph. 4:13-15)*

I think that the church is in need of this perfecting, edifying, maturing, and soundness in doctrine.

So what does the gift of apostle look like? The word *apostle* means "sent one." In Acts 13 we read:

"Now there were in the church that was at
Antioch certain prophets and teachers; as
Barnabas, and Simeon that was called Niger,
and Lucius of Cyrene, and Manaen, which had
been brought up with Herod the tetrarch, and
Saul. As they ministered to the Lord, and fasted,
the Holy Ghost said, Separate me Barnabas
and Saul for the work whereunto I have called
them. And when they had fasted and prayed,
and laid their hands on them, they sent them
away. So they, being sent forth by the Holy Ghost,
departed unto Seleucia; and from thence they
sailed to Cyprus." (Acts 13:1-4)

We see in this account the "sending" of Paul and Barnabas by the Holy Ghost. What follows is the most detailed account that we have in the scriptures of the life and ministry of two men who were called to be apostles. The following verse from Acts 14 clearly refers to both Paul and Barnabas as apostles:

"Which when the apostles, Barnabas and Paul,
heard of, they rent their clothes, and ran in
among the people, crying out. . . . " (Acts 14:14)

I believe the fulfillment of this ministry is manifested by the brother who goes into an area where the gospel is not known, begins to preach the gospel, and leads a few to Christ. He then disciples/nurtures that group until they have been established in the basic doctrines of the faith, having an understanding of how the church functions with the giftings that the Lord has given (this process is called "establishing" the church). After this he leaves that group, travels elsewhere, and continues a similar ministry. He may stay in contact with these groups and return to them some time later after the assembly has matured sufficiently when men who meet the qualifications of elder can be identified with the intention of helping them appoint elders.

We might say, "That seems to be describing what we call a missionary." Well, maybe and maybe not. Sometimes missionaries have a gift of helps, and they are going to the field to minister to some physical needs; or they may have a gift of teaching and are participating in discipleship ministry, etc. These are important ministries, but they are not an apostolic ministry.

We may, however, have someone go to the mission field, and whom we are calling a missionary, but who actually is fulfilling an apostolic ministry. I have known a few men over the many years that we have been meeting with believers who understand and believe in the ministry of the body, and who I believe have manifested this gifting. Not one of them have I ever heard refer to himself as an apostle, and these men might even be uncomfortable with that title. I am glad that this is the way it has been. As I mentioned before, we do not need to have a title or try to make it known to everyone what we believe our ministry is. We just need to be obedient to the Lord and let Him manifest the gifting according to His purpose and wisdom for us and for His church. It may be that someone will tell us someday how our ministry has blessed them, and we will begin to have some idea how we are being used. The effectiveness of our ministry is the real validation of our ministry. God has promised that the joints of the body will be compacted *"according to the effectual working in the measure of every part."*

God has promised the effectiveness of the gifting when the believer is obedient to minister in that gift. The last thing we need is an immature believer with a puffed-up image of himself who calls himself an apostle and attempts to usurp authority in the church based on his own impression of himself rather than exercising the genuine gifting of the Lord. The true gift of the Lord, when exercised, persuades humility rather than pride because we learn, as we obey, that the strength and effectiveness of the gifting is the Lord Himself.

I have written extensively on the gift of apostle because, even though it is likely to be the gift that we least often encounter, it is probably the gifting that is most likely to be misunderstood and misused.

2. PROPHET

The New Testament gift of prophet, which is for the church, is another gift that is often misunderstood and misused. When we think of the ministry of a prophet, we may think of men like Isaiah, Jeremiah, Ezekiel, etc., who were sent to minister to Israel under the Law. Their ministry was to be the Lord's spokesman in warnings, admonitions, rebukes, comforts, and revelations of things to come, etc., to a nation under the law. This prophetic ministry had a very different nature than the prophetic ministry that is a gift for the edification of the church. The ministering of the gift of prophet, in and for the church, may include warnings, admonitions, rebukes, and, occasionally, revelations of things to come; but the primary function of the prophet in the church is revealed to us in the following scripture: *"But he that prophesieth speaketh unto men to edification, and exhortation, and comfort" (1 Cor. 14:3).*

This gift may very well be the most common speaking gift given to the church. It is a very much needed and important gift for the edification and strengthening of the body—so much so that Paul exhorted the saints in Corinth as follows: *"Wherefore, brethren, covet to prophesy . . . "* (1 Cor. 14:39). This gift is also fairly easy to identify, compared to some others, both by its effect on the saints as well as by the believer himself who has the gift, as he discerns his consistent desire to edify, exhort, and comfort the saints.

3. Evangelist

Remember that these gifts have been given *"For the perfecting of the saints, for the work of the ministry, for the edifying of the body of Christ . . . "* (Eph. 4:12). We might think that a person with the gifting of evangelist is just someone who preaches the gospel, but I think this gift is something more than that. Certainly, the evangelist preaches the gospel; but since the gifting is for the edification of the body, I believe that the evangelist *gift* spoken of here refers to one who encourages, instructs, and exhorts the saints in evangelism.

4. Pastor

There has been a lot of confusion related to what a "pastor" is and what his ministry involves. Many seem to have concluded that a pastor is the ruling shepherd, primary overseer, and the main teacher of doctrine. He may have some elders working under him, but he makes the final decisions. He has likely been trained in a seminary that has fueled him with some incorrect notions about the gift of pastor. He does the majority of the speaking ministry, perhaps the majority of all ministry in the assembly, and, therefore, becomes the main "compactor" of the joints of the body. This is a great mistake and is definitely *not* what is taught in the New Testament concerning the function of the body of Christ. The only place where the word *pastor* is used in the New Testament is in Ephesians 4:11, where it is

listed as one of the five "gifts given unto men" for the edification of the saints.

"Pastor" is a gift, and many of those today who are being
called *pastor* may not even have the pastoral gifting. Those
who have this special gifting are inclined to come along-
side the saints and are concerned about their spiritual (and
perhaps physical) wellbeing. The saints are often drawn to
them, and find it easy to open up to them and share their
struggles. Those with a pastoral gift may be among ones
who speak from the pulpit, or they may not. Their ministry may be more one-on-one, perhaps with a family, some
young person, with a group of young people, or with the
elderly, etc. There may be several in a given assembly who
have a pastoral gifting.

Also, *pastor* and *elder/bishop/overseer* are not the same
thing. Pastor is a *supernatural* gifting, given by Christ to the
believer when he is saved. This gifting will be manifested as
the believer obeys the Lord in loving and serving the saints
and will be in effect the moment that he first obeys in faith.
On the other hand, the office, or responsibility, of elder/
bishop/overseer (which are all the same position) is not a
gift but is established by appointment, based upon mature
qualifications (see Titus 1:5-9). An elder may have a pastoral gift; he may have a teaching gift; he may be a prophet, an
evangelist, or have the gift of helps, etc. He must, by quali-
fication, be "apt to teach," which means that he handles the

Word well; he is sound in doctrine and capable of teaching but not necessarily exhibiting a full teaching gift/ministry.

The person with the gift of pastor is not necessarily one who has the responsibility of oversight. This would only be true if the man with the pastoral gift was also recognized and appointed as an elder. The responsibility for oversight is given to the elders. The scripture indicates a *plurality* of elders; there should always be more than one. The elders have the responsibility of guarding the flock against error, wolves in sheep's clothing, etc. They are also responsible to make sure that the saints are being fed and that the gifts are being encouraged and functioning. They may or may not be participating in the speaking ministries but will be responsible to make sure there is an environment that gives liberty, encourages the saints who have speaking ministries to grow in them, and ensures that all things are *"done decently and in order"* (1 Cor. 14:40).

The plurality of elders who understand their responsibility and are faithful in their shepherding and oversight is one of the major safeguards for the local assembly against error. When the assembly has only one man who is the main teacher, overseer, and guardian of sound doctrine, the whole assembly may go with him if he begins to go astray with his doctrine.

5. TEACHER

One with the gift of "teacher" will, obviously, be one who teaches the scriptures, not because it is his reluctant duty but because that is what he is in Christ. When he reads the Word, he will likely be given understanding of the sense and the application of what he is reading and have a strong desire to impart that to others.

Again, the test for the validity/reality of the gift is the *effectiveness* of his teaching. Are the saints growing not only in understanding of God's Word but also in application? One who is gifted by Christ as a teacher of the Word, will also have an unwavering commitment to teach truth. He will be quick to receive correction as soon as he is able to perceive that the correction is in accordance with the truth.

There are more gifts that could be discussed, but this is all we will look at for now.

Chapter Four

THE MEETING OF THE SAINTS

And they continued stedfastly in the apostles'
doctrine and fellowship, and in breaking
of bread, and in prayers. (Acts 2:42)

There is much instruction in this verse, which contains the core components for a valid, fruitful, power- ful, and blessed meeting of the saints. Let's examine the components:

1. THEY CONTINUED STEDFASTLY

They were fully committed to what they were doing together and desired to faithfully continue in these things.

Not forsaking the assembling of ourselves together, as the manner of some is; but exhorting one another: and so much the more, as ye see the day approaching. (Heb. 10:25)

We see from this scripture that it is important to the Lord that we are committed and consistent in meeting together with the saints.

2. IN THE APOSTLES' DOCTRINE

Since the New Testament, which reveals to us what the apostles taught, had not yet been written, their commitment to the "apostles' doctrine" would be equivalent to our being committed to the scriptures—reading the scriptures, meditating together on the scriptures, teaching and exhorting one another from the scriptures. What would be especially important for a new assembly would be to read through the New Testament together, focusing on what the apostles taught concerning the life and function of the church. For a beginning assembly, where there are not yet any brothers who are experienced in the speaking ministries, simply starting with reading from the scriptures would be important and also a blessing.

In fact, even with experienced speakers, *reading the scriptures* together is a great blessing. In our fellowship, which has been operating with the type of body ministry that we have been studying in the first three chapters of this series, after many years we continue to find reading a chapter of the Bible every meeting to be a great blessing as we go through the Bible together. All the men now in our fellowship have grown up in their ministries and are able ministers of the

Word; nevertheless we still read the scriptures together in our meeting and often find that much of the ministry is inspired out of the chapter that we read together. *Till I come, give attendance to reading, to exhortation, to doctrine* (1 Tim. 4:13).

3. AND FELLOWSHIP

The power of fellowship in Christ for the edification of believers cannot be overstressed. Before every meeting, those of us who arrive early for that purpose gather together for a few minutes to pray for our meeting. In that prayer time, we specifically ask the Lord to show Himself by working through each of us in everything that we do together. We ask that the Comforter lead us into all truth as we read the scriptures together. We ask the Lord to lead and speak through whoever stands to speak. We ask Him to lead us in the selection of hymns that we sing. We ask Him to help us in *"teaching and admonishing one another in psalms and hymns and spiritual songs . . . "* (Col 3:16). We ask Him to bless our fellowship together, guiding our conversations for the blessing of each other—that His power and blessing would be in a simple handshake. We always take a break approximately halfway through our meeting for about a half an hour. We have coffee and snacks and just enjoy a time of fellowship with one another. The Lord answers these simple prayers, and the saints are edified and growing in the knowledge of Him.

4. AND IN BREAKING OF BREAD

This, of course, refers to the communion remembrance. We do this when we come back from our break. This is a special time when our focus is on the Lord and remembering what He has done for us. We commit this remembrance to Him as we carry out the partaking of the elements in accordance with what has been written. This should be a special time of worship before the Lord.

5. AND IN PRAYERS

We always end our meeting with a time of intercessory prayer. We pray for our brethren in bonds, for our missionaries, for special prayer requests, and for one another.

I have shared with you much of how we order our meetings not because I wish to lay down some rule of order for you but only to offer some thoughts for you on how a meeting could be conducted. Trust the Lord to lead you and to be your strength as you minister to one another, and He will do so as you obey Him. My counsel is to start simple: pray, read the scriptures together, and break bread together. If any man has something on his heart to share, encourage him to share it even if it is just reading a verse or sharing a few words. Do not be discouraged but trust the Lord to make His strength perfect through your weakness. His power is not in the least restrained by our feeble efforts. He *"is able to do exceeding abundantly above all that we ask or think, according to the power that worketh in us"* (Eph. 3:20).

You will find that, as you continue to obey, the scriptures are being fulfilled. The body is edifying itself in love, and you are growing up in your ministry. As time goes on, you are able to bear witness of His strength with more confidence. It is also wonderful to see all of the members growing in their ministries. As the Lord leads each brother or sister in sharing the gospel with the lost, or as other likeminded believers find out about your fellowship, you may find your numbers growing. As the men grow in their speaking ministries, you may find, eventually, that you have two or more men who would like to speak during a given meeting. The scripture says: *"Let the prophets speak two or three, and let the other judge"* (1 Cor. 14:29). This is also one of the safeguards provided by the Lord in the ministry of the multiple giftings in the body. As the assembly grows in maturity, there may be men identified who meet the qualifications of elder and can be appointed to that position.

The scriptures make it clear that the public speaking-and-teaching portion of the meeting is given to the men, but that does not mean that the women's giftings or ministries are any less important than the men's. Women teaching other women; older women teaching younger women; women and mothers teaching children; women with gifts of mercy and/or helps, serving the body—no gift is less important than another in the body of Christ.

Once again, in these chapters, I have not covered all of the gifts; nor has this teaching been an exhaustive treatise on the church. Much more could be said, but hopefully this information may be an encouragement to those who would be in such a position that they are considering starting a church fellowship based from its beginning on simple obedience to what has been recorded for us in the New Testament.

PART TWO

"BEHOLD, I WILL DO SOMETHING NEW"

Pete Salas

Chapter Five

TO EVERY THING THERE IS A SEASON

To every [thing there is] a season, and a
time to every purpose under the heaven:
A time to be born, and a time to die; a
time to plant, and a time to pluck up [that
which is] planted (Ecclesiastes 3:1-2)

Having read *The Berean Call* throughout the years, I have noted many emails they have received from brothers and sisters acknowledging their plight and asking for help. Often their situation has drastically changed. After having been in a church for quite a few years, they now see their pastor, who once taught and followed the Word of God, deviating from it. Their most pressing question is *"Can you help us find a church in our area?"* This is the most common request we receive here at TBC, and it has been for more than two decades.

"BIBLICAL FELLOWSHIP IS HARD TO FIND"

My wife and I can identify with this question as we have experienced this same thing in the past. For years we've had a burden for our brothers and sisters who are struggling to find a solid Bible-based church or an assembly of believers with whom they could fellowship. In some places, it has been hard to find even two or three like-minded believers. We are truly living in a time when many are falling away from the faith. Nevertheless, the Lord is faithful to His own.

You will notice that some of the same false teachers/teachings that we encountered years ago are still prevalent today. In fact, many of them have come to full bloom and fruition. What was just beginning then is commonplace and acceptable now with scarcely a thought or question.

I am writing this to encourage others out there who find themselves in a situation similar to ours. As we eventually learned, we needed to remember to remind one another that we, as the Lord's sheep, are never without a Shepherd. God leads His dear people along. He said, *"My sheep hear My voice, and I know them, and they follow Me"* (John 10:27).

WALK BY FAITH, NOT BY SIGHT

We may be thinking that the Lord is far away and unaware of our circumstances when in reality He is *well* aware of our plight. Indeed, this is a time when we are to *"Walk by faith, not by sight"* (2 Cor. 5:7). We are to trust that God will do something new. As I read these words years ago, I knew that He spoke these very words first to His people, Israel. Yet I also believe that there is a spiritual application extended to us who are in the church. My wife and I saw the Lord do a wonderful thing in our life. He said, *"Remember ye not the former things, neither consider the things of old. Behold, I will do a new thing; now it shall spring forth; shall ye not know it? I will even make a way in the wilderness, and rivers in the desert"* (Isa. 43:18-19).

A DRASTIC CHANGE IN MINISTRY FOCUS

The Berean Call has been such a blessing to Margaret and me since its beginnings in the 90s. Prior to that, in 1986, I read *The Seduction of Christianity*, written by Dave Hunt and T. A. (Tom) McMahon, and I was blessed by their insights on humanistic psychology.

Dave and Tom had written to warn the church about how detrimental it would be to follow the teachings of psychology. In fact, psychology was one of the very teachings against which we were contending that had already crept into our own church. In addition, being in leadership at the church we attended, we understood that we were being introduced to Bill Hybels's "Seeker-Friendly" model. Our leaders told us that our church was going to begin implementing that approach to reaching the community.

Again, TBC helped us tremendously with this issue. The Lord gave us discernment and understanding to navigate through the issues that we had in front of us.

In 1991, we had exhausted all our options and had come to the realization that the church had taken a drastic turn in its ministry focus. Our senior pastor had retired and was being replaced with a young pastor who had been at the church for quite a few years. He was, however, not a "Bible man." Instead, he was an executive-minded pastor. Therefore, his emphasis was no longer on the exposition of the Word, as had been that of the previous pastor, but he and his pastoral staff began to teach and/or preach topical sermons, implementing many man-made devices. Ours was already a mega church, but he wanted to increase its size even more.

MEETINGS WITH OUR "MISSIONS PASTOR"

In spite of all that transpired, we never had contentious words with our pastors. We disagreed with what they were doing—and communicated that—but we loved the leaders to whom we were accountable. We simply saw that they were not turning back from the course on which they were headed. On several different occasions, I began to have meetings with each of the pastors who were my overseers. I spoke to my Missions Pastor, updating him about the Bible study that we were having in our home, letting him know how it was going. At the time, I was teaching from the gospel of Luke, and we were reaching out to those who were not yet believers. At one of our meetings, as we neared the end of our lunchtime, he brought up the subject of psychology. He knew my views on it, because I sometimes taught and warned of its dangers in the Sunday school class I was teaching. Again, I used this opportunity to share with him my views, but we did not agree.

Called on the Carpet

On another occasion, I was speaking with my Missions Pastor and my Peer Pastor, who headed up the 30-year-old marrieds group, both of whom I was under (where I taught Sunday School). They called me in on another issue relating to a guest speaker. We in leadership were notified that he would be speaking on the gospel throughout the week. Moreover, they wanted us to inform our classes so they could invite friends, family, and fellow workers to hear the gospel. Almost every year the church designated a week during which a guest evangelist would come and preach the gospel in order to reach the lost. It turned out that the man who was to speak this time was loosely titled the "Johnny Carson" of Christian speakers. He was a motivational speaker. That caught my attention. I began to observe things changing right before my eyes.

Unfortunately, this man did *not* preach the gospel to the many we had invited to hear him. I verbalized my concerns.

Needless to say, my pastors were not pleased with me. This man was from the Seeker-Friendly movement, and the preaching of the gospel was foreign to him!

At that time, they let me know that I, being in leadership, needed to be a "team player." They conveyed to me that "once we make a decision on something, we in leadership need to support that decision." Unfortunately, I could not.

Seeker-Friendly Model Implemented

The leaders stated that the meetings during which this man had spoken were successful because many people were inquiring about our church and the "Support Group Studies" that they were going to offer. Suffice it to say that these folks had not heard the gospel nor were they born again. Even so, they were welcomed into the church. This was the first time this approach had been implemented.

Without going into great detail, my "Missions Pastor" and my "30s Marrieds' Pastor" recommended that I speak with the "Evangelism Pastor" who had brought in about seven different "Support Group Studies" to reach these people.

Meeting with the Evangelism Pastor

I obtained these "studies" from the Evangelism Pastor. I looked them over and realized that *not one of them* had the gospel message in it. As I perused them, I saw that they had been written to make people "feel better about themselves" and to help them become "better people on a human level." They were "studies" on how to make your marriage better, etc., but they were devoid of the gospel, with no intention of reaching those who were lost! I shared my concern with the Evangelism Pastor, but to no avail.

Stepping Away from Man-Made Contracts and Psychology

There came a time when I had to step out of leadership in the Singles Ministry and the 30s Married Ministry, and finally the Gospel (evangelism) Outreach Ministry. I wasn't willing to compromise my convictions and teach something other than the Word of God. Nevertheless, the Lord was faithful to continue to open doors for His Word, and He gave us more light and direction. Through this, I learned that when someone decides not to compromise but purposes to walk in His light, He brings them into more light (which results in better discernment and understanding). *"...In Thy light shall we see light"* (Ps. 36:9b) and *"...The Word of God is not bound* [chained]*"* (2 Tim. 2:9).

Praying For and Seeking the Lord's Direction and Answer

In the several years during which all these things had transpired, my wife and I were praying for the Lord's direction. We knew the climate was changing and not for the good.

God answered our prayers when I had a conversation with my Missions Pastor.

Normally, we would have a monthly meeting where I would inform him about how the ministry was going. This time, at the end of our meal, he brought up the subject of psychology. He knew that I wasn't in agreement with what James Dobson and other "Christian psychologists" were teaching. He said to me, "I'm not telling you to do this, but if you're not happy here, you might want to look elsewhere."

I had been in that church 14 years and I had never been told that. He was a dear and kind man, and he didn't say it with any malice. However, at that moment, the Lord quickened me, and I knew that it was time to leave. God had answered our prayer. We had done all that we could do by trying to warn them. It was clear that they were not deviating from the plans and purposes they had devised for the church.

EXIT INTERVIEW WITH THE EXECUTIVE PASTOR

Last, but not least, I spoke with the Senior Executive Pastor. It is evident by that title that he was more of an executive than he was a biblical pastor. In fact, he was the one who was steering the ship off course. His father was likewise an executive in the business world. He lived in another state, but his influence on his son was strong. He wasn't even a part of our church but had been involved in the "Twelve Step Program" and apparently had been successful in his struggle with "alcoholism." Therefore, his son (our Executive Senior Pastor) was gung ho on implementing that program into the church, and he did. I spoke to him and notified him that we were leaving the church due to the issues I had mentioned. He, too, was a nice man and saw that we had made up our minds to go elsewhere. The Seeker-Friendly teachers had influenced the pastors to nicely coerce the people who were not in agreement with them to find another place where they would be happy. I am sure he was glad to see me go.

A Painful Departure

Sadly, after having attended that church for more than 14 years, we saw that the ship was going off course in dramatic fashion. Through much prayer and the leading of the Lord, we determined that He was leading us out of the church. While attending that church, I had been serving nearly the entire time, beginning with the music ministry and then moving into teaching the Bible. It was difficult to leave our friends with whom we had fellowshipped and had ministry.

False Doctrines Divide

Dave Hunt and Tom McMahon's *Berean Call* newsletters brought back many memories relating to our own experiences. (I'm not being psychological but just recounting what we went through back then.) The reason we left was that our pastors had parted from proclaiming the Word by adulterating it with manmade teachings and false doctrines. They were unwilling to forsake the direction in which they were heading. In addition, they were subtly suggesting to longtime members (as they had with us) that they look elsewhere for a church. Sometimes with others they were not so subtle.

WE LEFT NOT FOR A TRIVIAL MATTER BUT FOR FALSE TEACHING

I want to share this with whoever will listen. We did not leave because we didn't like the color of the pews or the carpet. It was not a trivial matter but rather a matter of the leadership teaching false doctrine. Sadly, we saw that the church was drifting away from the faith.

Chapter Six

IS HOME ASSEMBLY AN OPTION?

And let us consider one another to provoke unto love and to good works: not forsaking the assembling of ourselves together, as the manner of some [is]; but exhorting [one another]: and so much the more, as ye see the day approaching. (Hebrews 10:24-25)

Perilous Times Have Come

In these last of the last days of the church age, we know that perilous times have come *(2 Timothy 3:1-5, 1 Timothy 4:1)*. We are encountering things that many churches have experienced and have been going through for many years. Some are even meeting in homes and small meeting places due to the dying and deadness of many churches (Rev. 3:2). Don't get me wrong. I know there are still good Bible churches, and I am not encouraging a mad rush to home churches. A home meeting can be just as defective as any other church if its foundation is faulty.

Nonetheless, even some of the good Bible churches are deviating from their foundations. When their pastors go on to be with the Lord or retire, some of those who replace them are of an unsavory ilk. We live in different times, and we need to be ready to do the Lord's will to equip the saints who have no place to go—or someone else will. The home church might be a viable option for *some who have exhausted all their possibilities, or for some who believe that the Lord is directing them in that way.*

WHAT *IS* AND WHAT *IS NOT* FORSAKING OUR ASSEMBLING TOGETHER?

We were sad that we could no longer fellowship with some at our former church and also for the misunderstandings that some had of us and why we had left. However, we were not like those whom the writer of Hebrews addresses when he said *". . . Not forsaking the assembling of ourselves together, as the manner of some is"* (Heb. 10:25). It definitely was not that we no longer wanted to be part of a church meeting, but we knew that we must turn away from the proliferation of *false teaching*. It wasn't that we didn't want to "assemble...together" as a church. We simply saw the error and knew that we could no longer be around it. Could it be that "the manner of some" pastors, leaders, and assemblies are "forsaking" the Bible believer and not the other way around?

"The old principle is most true, that 'He is the schismatic who causes the separation, and not he who separates'" (J. C. Ryle). Our pastors had gone from teaching the Word to teaching doctrines of men and even of demons. We would have been foolish to continue in fellowship there: *"...For what fellowship hath righteousness with unrighteousness?"* (2 Cor. 6:14b).

Dealing with Any Bitterness before Moving Forward

Guilt can be foisted upon some because they have chosen to separate from their fellowship. Nevertheless, if they have exhausted all their options, have no root of bitterness, and *the Lord is leading them out*, then they have the liberty of the Lord to leave. If there is bitterness in one's heart, that needs to be addressed *before* leaving. However, if one has already left with bitterness, it still must be dealt with, or it will be carried right into the next fellowship and infect others adversely. (See Hebrews 12:15)

Wherever we go, we want to begin anew. *"Old things are passed away. . . ." "Forgetting those things which are behind, and reaching forth unto those things which are before"* (2 Cor. 5:17; Phil. 3:13).

WHEN DO WE WITHDRAW FROM THOSE ABANDONING THE SCRIPTURES?

Paul instructed Timothy as to what he should do if a church or a pastor was abandoning the Scriptures. He said, *"...From such withdraw."* First Timothy 6:3-5 tells us:

> *If any man teach otherwise, and consent not to wholesome words, even the words of our Lord Jesus Christ, and to the doctrine which is according to godliness; he is proud, knowing nothing, but doting about questions and strifes of words, whereof cometh envy, strife, railings, evil surmisings, perverse disputings of men of corrupt minds, and destitute of the truth, supposing that gain is godliness: from such withdraw thyself.*

THE RESULTING PLIGHT OF "PASTORS" / HIRELINGS SCATTERING THE SHEEP

Those who have withdrawn themselves and have written to TBC do not *want* to be without a church fellowship. The pastors and leaders have thrust them out because they simply wanted the pure milk of the Word. Their resulting sad situation is what is spoken of in Ezekiel 34:6, 21:

> *My sheep wandered through all the mountains, and upon every high hill: yea, my flock was*

scattered upon all the face of the earth, and
none did search or seek after them (v. 6) ....Ye
[pastors, leaders] have thrust with side and with
shoulder, and pushed all the diseased with your
horns, till ye have scattered them abroad (v. 21).

The first application applies to Israel. However, it has a secondary spiritual application to what is happening to the Lord's sheep in the church today.

There Is an Answer

I will refer you shortly to a *Q & A* in which Dave Hunt addresses this epidemic. He gives sound wisdom regarding what to look for when seeking an assembly. His words changed our view thirty years ago and have had a lasting effect on us to this day. I believe it would also help many today who are struggling with this same issue.

The Q & A That Laid the Foundation for a New Testament Assembly

In a 1988 *Q & A* section of *The Berean Call* newsletter, Dave delineated the way in which we should answer the inquiring believer's question. His response was also reprinted in October 2017. I truly believe that Dave Hunt had the wisdom of the Lord on this matter.

In the past, Dave had been part of an assembly that met in a home. In that gathering, they demonstrated what he described in the *Q & A*. Years later we observed it firsthand and participated in that same home assembly in like manner. Dave understood the simplicity of meeting in a group, whether large or small. The importance was not the size but the focus. He had the wisdom of the Lord on many other things as he implemented them into the ministry called The Berean Call (TBC). However, he also had an understanding of church life, which kept him grounded. We need to learn from others who have been through these kinds of situations and have come into something new that the Lord has ordained. We also want to learn from those to whom the Lord has given new insights concerning their experiences.

THE BEREANS POSE A QUESTION
PERTAINING TO THEIR DILEMMA

In one of his newsletters, Tom McMahon quoted a question someone sent to him concerning finding a church. He or she wrote, "Dear Brothers and Sisters at The Berean Call—I'm at wit's end. We recently moved to a new community, and we can't find a church that is teaching God's Word without adding to it or subtracting from it. Do you know of any good churches in our area?"

To the Berean-minded believer, this is of utmost importance. They find themselves in a situation in which they have never been before and are perplexed—they have no place where they can find fellowship. Having gone back and evaluated what we went through in 1988, I remember Dave encouraging those who were also struggling with their current churches. Following is a composite of several similar questions: "We can't seem to find a church in our area that has godly leadership and biblical preaching. We feel so alone and now just read the Bible and pray at home. What should we do? And how do we find a 'good' church?"

Back then, Dave's response helped me and another brother to get our focus on the Lord's will and way as to how to begin a meeting ourselves. I also had been studying the Book of Acts and the origins of the church. I had other like-minded believers who demonstrated what Dave describes in his response to the person who asked the question. I would like to share that with you all because I believe it will bring a blessing to you. It pertains to Dave Hunt, and I will share that further on in this booklet.

Chapter Seven

TIME TO ABANDON SHIP

Many biblical believers are finding themselves in a situation similar to those on the *Titanic* more than a century ago—and the ship is going down. The churches where they once worshiped and served are now being inundated with water from a polluted stream. The water is rising up over them. Although their desire has always been to serve, they are beginning to realize that their service will not benefit those who are happy to remain in a sinking ship flooded with false teachings. Now, their only desire is to somehow get off that ship!

CULTIVATING DISCERNMENT

The Lord our Shepherd has warned us: *"And Jesus answered and said unto them, Take heed that no man deceive you"* (Mat. 24:4). He also said *"And ye shall know the truth and the truth shall make you free"* (John 8:32). The Lord calls us to be discerning, and Paul likewise tells us how the Holy Spirit cultivates discernment. He says:

> But God hath revealed them [His Word] unto us by his Spirit: for the Spirit searcheth all things, yea, the deep things of God. . . . But he that is spiritual judgeth [discerns] all things, yet he himself is judged of no man" (1 Cor. 2:10 & 15).

Paul also tells us *"Stand fast therefore in the liberty where-with Christ hath made us free, and be not entangled again with the yoke of bondage"* (Gal. 5:1).

Cultivating discernment also comes by making *choices* to stand in the liberty Christ attained for us so that we will not entangle ourselves with man-made doctrines and aberrant teachings that will foist upon us a burden of bondage.

Evacuating the Life Blood from the Church

A few years after we had left the church of which we had once been a part, we learned that the Executive Pastor had made a decision that they would no longer mention the blood of Christ in the church service when he preached (*see Mark 8:38*). Concerning the blood of Christ, he told the congregation, "Though this is precious to us, the unchurched would say 'Yuck! What's that?'" He had completely taken them into a Seeker-Friendly approach and removed these folks, and others who would come, from the only thing that could save them, that is, the blood of Christ!

The Bible makes it clear: "...*Without shedding of blood is no remission [forgiveness, pardon]*" (Heb. 9:22b). Sadly, their aim was to bring in the lost and focus on what *pleased* them. The concern was no longer for the believer's growth. To remain in—or to send someone back into—a church that is apostatizing is detrimental to one's faith. In addition, if they have their family with them, they, too, will be infected with apostate teaching.

Doctrinal Deficiency
Leads to False Practices

A sister from our fellowship has neighbors (a couple) whom we knew from our former church. They are dear people. They recently left the church that we had been in some 28 years ago. My question here was rhetorical: *How was their spiritual maturity these days?* Well, the wife was taking trips to Redding, California (Bethel Church), to receive "healing" for her back ailments. There's no telling what else she was receiving there from the laying on of hands. Unfortunately, we just found out that she also was diagnosed with cancer and recently passed away. I say this with great sadness.

We need to realize that false teaching and false practices will stunt the growth of a genuine believer. These teachings prohibit one from developing discernment, which will cause them to follow the latest "wind of doctrine" (Eph. 4:14). In addition, the unbiblical laying on of hands can pass on a demonic influence. We once ministered to a young man who had lost all control of his bodily functions as a result of a well-known preacher having laid hands on him. Both the man and the preacher thought it was a work of the Holy Spirit when in fact it was a false spirit! Recognizing what someone is teaching will indicate what kind of fruit will come forth.

LISTENING TO THE SHEPHERD'S VOICE AND HIS WORD ONLY!

We believers need to adhere to our Shepherd's voice/His Word. He tells us *"My sheep hear my voice, and I know them, and they follow me... And when he putteth forth his own sheep, he goeth before them, and the sheep follow him: for they know his voice. And a stranger will they not follow, but will flee from him: for they know not the voice of strangers"* (John 10:27; vv. 4,5).

If the sheep are following the Shepherd, He will lead them into truth, and they will find safety. He will lead them out of danger, giving them an awareness of what surrounds them. That is why they (and their pastors) should be concerned about the voices they're listening to (radio, television, and the internet) and pay attention to where their pastors and teachers are leading them.

Recognizing the Stranger's Voice and Fleeing from It

John 10:5a states: *And a stranger will they not follow...* A true believer knows they are not to follow "a stranger," and they demonstrate it by an act of obedience to the Lord. We deceive ourselves by thinking that just because we *recognize* false teaching, it's still okay to stay in and around it. This is one of the most misleading and naïve assumptions one can make. Knowing that we are not to follow a stranger must be *lived out by the obedience of faith.* We have to get up and *out* of there or we really haven't learned the truth that the Lord is trying to teach us. It's not enough to simply know it in our minds, but it must also reach into our *hearts*, bringing forth the conviction that affects our will.

Our Lord tells us that His sheep "...will flee from him [the stranger]" (John 10:5a). This is the most normal response for sheep (believers). We must flee from the false teachers who continue to persist in teaching their lies, even though they have been warned to stop!

I believe that if we don't try to dissuade a believer from remaining or going back into the error from which they've come out, they will eventually become insensitive and unresponsive to the error. They may think they have it all under control, yet it begins to change their thinking. "Wherefore let him that thinketh he standeth take heed lest he fall." (1 Cor. 10:12)

*"Ye did run well; who did hinder you
that ye should not obey the truth?"(Gal. 5:7)*

*"Trust in the LORD with all thine heart; and lean
not unto thine own understanding." (Prov. 3:5)*

***"Blessed is the man that walketh not
in the counsel of the ungodly**, nor standeth
in the way of sinners, nor sitteth in the seat
of the scornful." (Ps. 1:1)*

OLD THINGS ARE PAST; ALL THINGS ARE NEW

When we first come to the Lord, we immediately recognize that we no longer want to live the way we used to and we gladly turn away from the old life by an act of faith. As we continue to walk with the Lord, we turn away from anything that would take us away from Him. This is especially crucial in these perilous times.

BEREANS HAVE LEARNED TO DISCERN

Since the beginning of The Berean Call ministry, Dave Hunt and Tom McMahon's main objective has been to cultivate an environment for believers to learn discernment and to act upon it. TBC's mission statement clearly delineates this. (I encourage you to read their statement on The Berean Call website). Because of what they purposed, there is a group of Berean believers who now recognize danger when they see it. They have been persuaded by the Word to follow the Lord in the things He has taught them. Bereans have developed discernment and respond to the pressing danger. Their ears perk up when they distinguish someone else's voice other than that of our Lord. He says "...*for they know not the voice of strangers*" (John 10:5b). Attuned to His Word, they hear the stranger's voice and can detect it immediately—for example, Sarah Young's "Jesus" from her book *Jesus Calling*. That indeed is a stranger's voice, and they "... will flee from him."

No Desire to Acquire Discernment

Conversely, how many times have all of us seen believers who appear to have no discernment, nor any desire to acquire it? They remain ignorant of the imminent danger of aberrant teaching and the calamity that lies ahead. Their lives could possibly be set adrift, as Paul warned: "...*Some having put away concerning faith have made shipwreck*" (1 Tim. 1:19b). We are saddened by their unwillingness to recognize that they are vulnerable to much error and yet entirely unaware of it. We are told in Proverbs 19:2a: "*Also, that the soul be without knowledge, it is not good....*" In addition, Paul tells the believers in 1 Corinthians 15:34: "*Awake to righteousness, and sin not; for some have not the knowledge of God: I speak this to your shame.*"

This Is No Time for Despair

We, as His sheep, are not without hope. We must look to the Lord and believe that He can and will do something new. That is how Margaret and I looked at it when we were experiencing these things back in 1991. Moreover, the Lord met us! We understood that this was no time for despair. Those out there who may be going through this now can be encouraged, as Margaret and I were. Look to the Lord and hear Him say:

> *"Remember ye not the former things, neither consider the things of old. Behold, I will do a new thing; now it shall spring forth; shall ye not know it? I will even make a way in the wilderness, and rivers in the desert." (Isa. 43:18-19)*

Our Shepherd Leads and Feeds Us

Though hirelings and wolves in sheep's clothing forsake us, our Shepherd, our Lord, will take us up; He will lead us to new pastures; He will feed us and draw us ever closer to Him than before. (See Ps. 23:1-6)

By God's grace, that is what He did with us. We can testify of that. He deepened our faith and understanding, drew us nearer to Him than ever before, and brought forth a fountain overflowing with joy and rejoicing within our hearts.

We desire to share that with our brothers and sisters who feel like they are all alone. Nevertheless, each one must come to that place where he or she believes that the Lord will do a new thing. The Scriptures say, *". . . For He hath said, [and we must believe] I will never leave thee nor forsake thee"* (Heb. 13:5b).

Coming back to what Dave Hunt wrote in the *Q & A* section about finding a church, the Question was a composite of several similar questions: *"We can't seem to find a church in our area that has godly leadership and biblical preaching. We feel so alone and now just read the Bible and pray at home. What should we do? And how do we find a 'good' church?"*

First-century Church Life

Dave's response helped us tremendously to re-evaluate First-century New Testament church/assembly life in light of the Book of Acts. This is codified in Acts 2:42, which describes what the believers did. Luke tells us:

"And they continued stedfastly in the apostles' doctrine and fellowship, and in breaking of bread, and in prayers." This was the foundation laid at the beginning of the early Church, the ensuing Pentecost, and this is also how we began our assembly!

Two or Three Gathered in His Name?

Dave then replies, "It is a sad commentary on the state of the church that we receive many such queries." What marks a "healthy" church? Crucial to the answer is Matthew 18:20: *"For where two or three are gathered together in my name, there am I in the midst of them."*

Is Dave saying that a "healthy" fellowship may comprise only two or three believers? Well, we were in a church that had 3,500 members, and it became an unhealthy apostate church.

My wife and I know brothers and sisters who simply meet with two or three because in their small town there is no church that is sound in doctrine. Neither the amount of persons nor the program it has is the primary issue. So what *is* the primary issue? What is the central focus?

As Dave stated: *"Christ* himself must be the central focus—not a pastor, gripping sermons, a strong missionary emphasis, exciting youth programs, compatible fellow members, or even agreeable doctrines—important as all these factors are."

Chapter Eight

TRANSITIONING TO CHRIST AS THE CENTRAL FOCUS

I am going to go back to 1989 up to 1991, when we were contending against the teachings of psychology, self-esteem, and the seeker-friendly implementation into the church. I'm going to share how the Lord used Dave to help us and give us some direction. I was still teaching Sunday School and had a weekly gospel outreach in our home. We were reaching out to the people within our community.

One of the elderly couples in our study brought a missionary couple (who had ministered in the Amazon rain forest of Peru) to our study one summer evening. They had been there for 40-plus years, had just retired, and had come home to a town near us. It didn't take us long to recognize that this couple had a love for the Lord. I would often think that *he* should have been teaching our Bible study instead of me. Neil was a humble man, and it was evident that he had lived a life that was yielded to the Lord. At 84 years of age, they both had such sweet spirits about them. There came a time when I briefly shared with him about the struggle we were going through at our church. I asked him and his wife to pray for us. They were not a part of our church nor did they mention the church they attended.

Finally, Margaret and I made the decision to come out of our church yet purposed not to go church shopping/hopping but just to pray and get the Lord's direction. Therefore, I called our missionary friends and let them know we had left our church and to please pray for us. Shortly after, he called me and asked if he and an elder from their assembly could come and visit us. We said yes and that next Wednesday they visited us. Even though they had known us for a few years, for the elder's sake, they asked us to give our testimonies as to how we came to know the Lord. We were glad to share how He had saved us. They then invited us to their Lord's Day meeting.

The meeting was in a home on the outskirts of Turlock, California. The property was surrounded by an inviting peach orchard. It was a beautiful older home owned by a farmer and his wife. The husband had passed on. His wife, however, continued the weekly meeting, and our brother Neil and his wife were a part of that gathering along with about ten other believers and the elder and his wife. The beauty and simplicity of the meeting was like nothing we had seen before.

The Centerpiece of the Meeting

The meeting began with worshipping the Lord. The hymns we sang were solely focused on God Himself. They had no instruments, but they were not averse to having any; they just didn't have a musician there. Nevertheless, the worship was sweet.

Dave Hunt wrote about the importance of worship. He stated that "A fervent love for Christ and a heartfelt corporate worship of His Person must be the primary mark of a healthy church. The early church was thus characterized."

But the hour cometh, and now is, when the true worshippers shall worship the Father in spirit and in truth: for the Father seeketh such to worship him. (John 4:23)

This gathering of believers that Margaret and I met with demonstrated what Dave described. With no song leader nor worship team nor pastor they worshipped the Lord from the Scriptures, with song and prayerful offerings (1 Pet. 2:5; Heb. 13:15).

Dave also said of the first-century church, "It met regularly on the first day of the week in remembrance of [Christ's] death.

That weekly outpouring of praise, worship, and thanksgiving had one purpose—to give God His due portion."

When we came to this part of the meeting, "The breaking of bread," known by many as communion, I witnessed something I had never seen. The men in the meeting, whoever was willing, individually stood up and read a scripture that recalled the Lord Jesus Christ in His death, burial, and resurrection. He then would offer up praise, worship, adoration, and thanksgiving to the Father for sending His Son. After he sat down, another would stand and do the same. Throughout this part of the meeting, we continued to sing worshipful hymns. There was no one officiating or orchestrating the meeting. Yet, by the leading of the Holy Spirit, there was order. There was nothing ecstatic or out of control, only a simplicity and beauty in worship and remembrance of the Lord Jesus (Ps. 29:2). Christ truly was in the midst (Matt. 18:20).

All I could think within myself was "*This* is what I've been missing!" It was indeed life changing to me. I witnessed a wonderful worship time orchestrated by the Spirit giving the Lord Jesus all the glory.

WHY AM I SHARING THIS?

You might be saying, "Why are you telling us this?" There is a reason, and I'm getting to it. After that portion of the meeting, we took a short break for coffee and a snack and some fellowship. I had a conversation with the hostess of the meeting. Her name was Shamira. We were talking about authors, and I mentioned Dave Hunt's name.

I was surprised when she said she knew of a Dave Hunt who had been part of their meeting there in that home years ago. I told her that he had written a number of books. She responded, "He's written one that I know of." I was sure that this could not be the same Dave Hunt. She took me to her bookshelf and pulled out a book that Dave had written years before.

I was stunned that in that very house on the outskirts of Turlock, Dave and Ruth Hunt had been part of that small meeting many years before. This is not to exalt Dave but to show the sovereign hand of God in this. Dave, at that time, was still working in the corporate world and had come from Los Angeles to Merced to help turn around a company that was struggling financially. Merced was not far from Turlock. So not only was Dave helping us by what he had written at TBC, describing to the couple in the *Q & A* the primary importance in a meeting, but now, here we were, in the home where they had once worshipped and been in fellowship! It was as if he were describing that meeting in the *Q & A*! Now, years later, this is what Margaret and I witnessed in that home assembly that morning.

There were more than "two or three. . . ." There were ten or eleven. Yet to this day, that meeting changed Margaret's and my life, and we patterned our future meetings after that. Once again, we had found encouragement from Dave and TBC when we had not many to turn to. The *Lord* led us to a meeting that exemplified what Dave described to a tee in the newsletter! After our short break of fellowship, we commenced again. We sang more hymns, went through the Scriptures verse by verse, and, again, it was a blessing. We ended with a time of prayer.

OF MOST IMPORTANCE: WORSHIP!

Dave's perspective on the believers meeting together helped change my mind on what was of most importance. When he said, "Christ himself must be the central focus," he meant that worship of the Lord was of primary importance. The Lord was to be exalted. It was evident that this was Dave's heart's desire throughout the years. He was drawing from the Book of Acts, chapter two. Dave said, "What stirred them (the first century Church) was a fervent love for Christ and a heartfelt corporate worship of His Person. [That] must be the *primary mark* of a healthy church. The early church was thus characterized.... That weekly outpouring of praise, worship, and thanksgiving had one purpose—to give God His due portion."

Dave continued, ". . . It isn't primarily a matter of my need, my edification, my enjoyment, or my spiritual satisfaction, but of His worth in my eyes and the eyes of the church."

Secondary Focus: Servanthood

Dave makes it very clear to this couple inquiring in the *Q & A* as to what to look for in a biblically sound and healthy church or assembly. He then describes what follows worship: "As I see it, our secondary focus should be our opportunity for servanthood with a corporate body of believers." To rearrange the order of this is to elevate service over worship, and then man becomes the emphasis and not the Lord. Many churches have confused the order to the point of not knowing what worship of the Father and the Son is. It is important to know whom and why we are serving, and that flows from first knowing whom it is that we worship (1 Pet. 2:5,9).

Dave then continued, "I give myself to a needy, imperfect people for whom I can pray, for whose needs I can concern myself in practical ways, to whom I can be an encourager and a minister of the Word, and among whom I can demonstrate and work out Christ's desire that His own 'might be one.' This fellowship is commanded: *'Not forsaking the assembling of ourselves together"* (Heb. 10:25). Is it our joy to gather with God's people in intercessory prayer and study of the Word, or is Sunday-morning-only quite enough? *A healthy church will not only gather unto Him, but with each other."*

Dave shares here that we are not to neglect service within the church but we must simply prioritize it. It is very important that we worship the Lord and minister one to another in love.

"*And he* [a certain lawyer who was testing Jesus] *answering, said* [to Jesus], *Thou shalt love the Lord thy God with all thy heart, and with all thy soul, and with all thy strength, and with all thy mind* [worship]*; and thy neighbour as thyself"* [service] (Luke 10:27).

In summing up his answer in the *Q & A*, Dave says once again, "Remember, however, the order of priority: worship—(do you worship sincerely, wholeheartedly, and in a manner satisfying to the object of that worship?) The final decision as to your church affiliation must be, prayerfully, yours. Is your personal worship of the Savior so joyful and satisfying a thing both to you and to Him that it supersedes other considerations?

Do your opportunities for service render your fellowship sufficiently meaningful and significant? Or do doctrinal concerns or lack of biblical preaching and teaching cancel out the other two? You must seek the Lord for His answer. God's comforting assurance remains: 'For where two or three are gathered together in my name, there am I in the midst of them.'"

Dave gives the reader things they should consider concerning worship and serving: "Or do doctrinal concerns or lack of biblical preaching and teaching cancel out the other two?" Then he says, "You must seek the Lord for His answer. God's comforting assurance remains: *'For where two or three are gathered together in my name, there am I in the midst of them.'"*

How Dave's Focus Helped
to Change Our View on Worship

What I came to realize is that Dave's pinpoint focus on worship is what gave him spiritual clarity of thought in his writings, his talks, his videos, and on the radio. Everything started from above (Col. 3:1-2): *"If ye then be risen with Christ, seek those things which are above, where Christ sitteth on the right hand of God. Set your affection on things above, not on things on the earth."*

That brought light and understanding to the issues he was addressing pertaining to the Church and the world. I was much encouraged by what Dave had written. Not only that, but the Lord gave us a view into how he and Ruth worshipped. That was invaluable for us to see and partake in. We not only agreed with what Dave wrote, but now we came to agree with how he worshipped also.

DAVE'S ADVERSITY BROUGHT FORTH
SPIRITUAL FORTITUDE

What the Lord worked in Dave Hunt brought forth a spiritual fortitude that enabled him to face adversity from not only the world but also from his own brethren who vilified and misunderstood him. Their own assembly ostracized him and Ruth. They went through the pain of separation. It caused them to draw closer to the Lord when even their brothers and sisters forsook them. However, the Lord took them up (Ps. 27:10).

Through this adversity, the Lord strengthened Dave to stand alone with Him. That is why years later he could write words of encouragement to those asking the question in the *Q & A*—words that still stand in the face of today's apostasy when some leaders have driven believers from their church meetings on purpose. We need men and women who have walked through hardship and have come through victoriously and with understanding.

> *Wisdom is the principal thing; therefore get wisdom: and with all thy getting get understanding (Prv 4:7).*

> *But thanks be to God, which giveth us the victory through our Lord Jesus Christ (1 Cor. 15:57).*

Chapter Eight

A BOLD MOVE TO BEGIN ON A NEW FOUNDATION

Today, as some are coming out of heresy-riddled churches, they could simply meet as the Lord said, *"For where two or three are gathered together in my name there am I the midst of them"* (Matt. 18:20). He set the parameters. We began to meet in similar fashion. Quite possibly the Lord could begin a new assembly using those coming out of these churches. They could begin anew on a solid foundation.

"For other foundation can no man lay than that is laid, which is Jesus Christ" (1 Cor. 3:11; Matt. 7:24-25; 2 Tim. 2:19). Another possibility is that for a short duration they could meet this way until the Lord leads them to a sound Bible-teaching church. He can do many things if we only trust Him that He will. However, to stay in or return to an apostate fellowship should not be an option. We are given numerous

commands and admonitions to *come out*, to *come away*, to *turn away*, to *flee*, to *mark and avoid*, to *withdraw from*, and to *follow not . . . evil*.

WHO WE ARE IN CHRIST

I would like us to look at a few scriptures in light of this subject. Some people are hesitant to leave their churches because of uncertainty and fear of the unknown. Paul tells us *"For God has not given us the spirit of fear; but of power, and of love, and of a sound mind"* (2 Tim. 1:7). The Lord will give us His strength and His boldness and confidence if we just trust and obey Him: *". . . In whom we have boldness and access with confidence by the faith of Him"* (Eph. 3:12). *"Be strong in the Lord, and in the power of His might"* (Eph. 6:10).

PAUL URGES US TO SPIRITUAL AWARENESS

Romans 16:17-18: *"Now I beseech you, brethren, mark them which cause divisions and offenses contrary to the doctrine which ye have learned; and avoid them. For they that are such serve not our Lord Jesus Christ, but their own belly; and by good words and fair speeches deceive the hearts of the simple."*

Paul says we are to *"mark them,"* which means to scope them out and *"avoid them,"* or, *"to go out of the way, or to turn away."* This includes the pastor or leader who is teaching false doctrine along with those who are following him.

Paul Shows Us What Not to Do and What We Are to Do

Be ye not unequally yoked together with unbelievers: for what fellowship hath righteousness with unrighteousness? and what communion hath light with darkness? And what concord hath Christ with Belial? or what part hath he that believeth with an infidel? And what agreement hath the temple of God with idols? For ye are the temple of the living God; as God hath said, I will dwell in them, and walk in them; and I will be their God, and they shall be my people. Wherefore come out from among them, and be ye separate, saith the Lord, and touch not the unclean thing; and I will receive you. And will be a Father unto you, and ye shall be my sons and daughters, saith the Lord Almighty. (2 Cor. 6:14-18)

Having therefore these promises, dearly beloved, let us cleanse ourselves from all filthiness of the flesh and spirit, perfecting holiness in the fear of God. (2 Cor. 7:1)

Margaret and I had recognized the apostasy in our church nearly thirty years ago and came out of it as the Lord directed us by His Word and His Spirit.

ENCOURAGING ONE ANOTHER
AS THE DAY DRAWS NEAR

In the early days, I often wondered why the Lord brought us out in the way that He did, but over the last 15 years or so, I began to see the reason more clearly. By His grace, He has given us opportunity to minister to brothers and sisters who are thinking of leaving their churches, and to others who are without church fellowship and in need of encouragement and direction.

THAT NO FLESH SHOULD GLORY IN HIS PRESENCE

We recognize who we are and are in agreement with what our Lord said in John 15:5c: *"For without Me ye can do nothing."* Likewise, we identify with what the apostle Paul said,

> *"For ye see your calling, brethren, how that not many wise men after the flesh, not many mighty, not many noble, are called: But God hath chosen the foolish things of the world to confound the wise; and God hath chosen the weak things of the world to confound the things which are mighty; And base things of the world, and things which are despised, hath God chosen, yea, and things which are not, to bring to nought things that are: That no flesh should glory in his presence" (1 Cor. 1:26-29).*

We simply walked by faith and had an expectation and confidence that God would do something new for His sheep. Every believer can have that same mindset and glorify the Lord.

By the Spirit, Paul looks down the corridor of time and tells us what will be taking place in the last days, which we are experiencing at this time. He says:

> *This know also, that in the last days perilous times shall come. For men shall be lovers of their own selves, covetous, boasters, proud, blasphemers, disobedient to parents, unthankful, unholy, without natural affection, trucebreakers, false accusers, incontinent, fierce, despisers of those that are good, traitors, heady, highminded, lovers of pleasures more than lovers of God; having a form of godliness, but denying the power thereof: from such turn away.*
> *(2 Tim. 3:1-5)*

I first learned these scriptures from The Berean Call. Dave and Tom were way ahead of many in seeing what was infiltrating the churches. This is the reason why I am writing this. I am simply saying that the urgency of the day should prompt an immediate response to the Scriptures because of the perilous times and the subtlety of deceptions. Many believers are in the situation that Paul is describing. He is not suggesting that we remain where the error is proliferating.

Concerning false teachers he says, *"Having a form of god-liness, but denying the power thereof: from such turn away."* We are to turn away, avoid, and shun them. We are living in the days when our brothers and sisters in Christ should have heightened awareness through the Lord's Word and the guidance of the Holy Spirit. We need to hear God's Word and obey it.

> *Then spake Jesus again unto them, saying, I am the light of the world: he that followeth me shall not walk in darkness, but shall have the light of life. (John 8:12)*

THE LORD LEADS US OUT OF DARKNESS INTO HIS LIGHT

As He said, *"He that followeth me shall not walk in darkness."* The time for believers to draw near to the Lord and follow Him more closely is now. They also need to find fellowship with likeminded believers and minister to one another. However, it might be in a new way, outside of what they have previously known. That is what the Lord did with us as we followed Him. In addition, we are to continue to go out and share the gospel with the lost, hoping that they will be saved, and then discipling them when they do come to the Lord.

Both Men and Women Had the Opportunity to Share the Gospel

The men in our fellowship went to the gospel mission, preached the gospel, and ministered to the men there. In the same way, the women from our fellowship went to the women's mission and shared the gospel, leading some to the Lord. This also led to a Bible study with them.

I Will Build My Church

We are told by our Lord, *"And I say also unto thee...I will build my church; and the gates of hell shall not prevail against it"* (Matt. 16:18).

The Lord sent the Holy Spirit on the day of Pentecost, and He promised Peter that he would receive the keys of the kingdom of heaven, which was the gospel. That is what Peter preached, and *"The same day there were added unto them about three thousand souls"* (Matt. 16:19; Acts 2:41). Thus, the Lord began something new and powerful: His church!

Today, it seems as though the Lord is bringing His Church back to its foundation, which is to meet in simple fashion, as Luke described in the Book of Acts, chapter two: *"And they continued stedfastly in the apostles' doctrine and fellowship, and in breaking of bread, and in prayers"* (v. 42).

It's Not the Size of the Meeting but the Spiritual Vibrancy of It

Do not misunderstand me. I am not saying that there's going to be another Pentecost. The Lord is simply calling some of His people to meet in a fresh new way, unencumbered by fluff and programs that they may have been accustomed to in the past. Maybe you won't be in a church of 1,000 people, or even 100. It could be as small as 10 or fewer. We left a church that had 3,500 members, to meet initially with a group of seven or eight people, which continued to grow.

The Early Church Meetings Were in Homes

Remember when Peter preached, and 3,000 were saved? There were no coliseums, no stadiums, no synagogues, and no church structures where all those people could meet. So what did they do? They met in the temple for a time, until persecution came from the Jews. Then we are told that the apostles met *"from house to house," "and in every house,"* with many of the new believers (Acts 2:46; 5:42).

"And they, continuing daily with one accord in the temple, and breaking bread from house to house, did eat their meat with gladness and singleness of heart" (Acts 2:46); *"And daily in the temple, and in every house, they ceased not to teach and preach Jesus Christ."* (Acts 5:42)

What an exciting time they all had, experiencing something new that the Lord had begun! It was something wonderful and powerful. They were enjoying their new life, free from sin and growing in the grace and knowledge of our Lord and Savior Jesus Christ!

By God's Word, We Are to Reevaluate Our Situation

What is taking place in our time is that the Lord is causing His people to reevaluate what is of utmost importance. I am confident that the Lord has placed The Berean Call in a great place to continue to reach those who desire to be ready for the Lord's coming.

 Some believers are not longing for a "new way," nor are they looking for "new paths." We are looking for what the prophet described in Jeremiah 6:16: *"Thus saith the Lord, Stand ye in the ways, and see, and ask for the old paths, where is the good way, and walk therein, and ye shall find rest for your souls. But they said, we will not walk therein."*

We, as His people are wanting to *"Stand...in the ways, and see, and ask for the old paths, where is the good way, and walk therein."* Nevertheless, at this time many are choosing to do otherwise and are departing from the faith. Jeremiah tells us, *"But they said, we will not walk therein."* Contrary to this statement, we say, *"We* will *walk therein."*

Chapter Nine

BEGINNING ANEW
WITH JOYFUL ANTICIPATION

G oing back to October of 1991, and to what I described earlier of having observed the worship and remembrance meeting of which Dave Hunt had been a part, Margaret and I, along with a few likeminded believers, began meeting in similar fashion. The Lord had already prepared each one of us. He initiated something new and unexpected.

He established our first meeting, and one of our sisters recounted to me recently her joyful anticipation over what the Lord was going to do. A brother read from Isaiah 40:31: *"But they that wait upon the Lord shall renew their strength; they shall mount up with wings as eagles; they shall run, and not be weary; and they shall walk, and not faint."*

We were encouraged by what he shared—to wait and see what the Lord was going to do. We sang hymns, prayed together, broke bread, and studied His Word.

Our meeting extended beyond what we expected. There was joyful fellowship as we sensed the presence of the Lord in our midst.

WE MET FOR HALF A YEAR IN THIS MANNER, AND THEN...

We continued to meet in our home on Friday nights for 26 weeks. The meeting continued to grow. Don Avigliano, who was a part of our fellowship, wrote a book in 1995 titled *The Alternative Church.* This book describes the beginnings of something new the Lord originated among us. Don said, "We had all come to realize that God was doing more than just having us meet for extra fellowship and encouragement. So, on Resurrection Sunday, April 19, 1992, we had our first Lord's day meeting."

The following is a quote from *The Alternative Church: An Experience of New Testament Christianity Following the Pattern of the First Century Church.*

The Author's Preface

"In the autumn of 1991, a group of Christians met. They were questioning some things they were encountering in the religious systems of the traditional churches. They were led by the Lord to meet for fellowship outside the traditional churches. As others have done before, they sought to worship their Lord and Savior, Jesus Christ, in spirit and in truth. This is the story of how the Lord took that beginning and spiritually developed it into a unique fellowship—one patterned after the early church that we read about in the Book of Acts. This is the story of that fellowship, how it came about, and how it developed. It is ironic that what is closest to the early church must be presented as an *alternative* form of church life—but this is the situation in which we find ourselves in our time of increasing apostasy!" — *Don Avigliano, 1995*

I am sharing this for the simple reason that I want to show how the Lord took a group of believers who solely desired to follow Him and His Word by His grace. He honored our meager attempt. We had felt the pressure to compromise in the church with the programs they offered. We didn't want to participate in many of the things they were implementing.

For instance, Larry Crabb's book, *Inside Out* (which is humanistic psychology amalgamated with the Bible), and also, "friendship contracts," "relationship contracts" (which recommended following man's reasoning and promoted legalism). In addition to these were the TJTA (Taylor

Johnson Temperament Analysis) personality test, and support groups that I have already mentioned earlier.

We understand and we empathize with what our brothers and sisters are going through. They are writing to TBC because of the pressure they are experiencing to compromise their convictions. The inundation of error and deceptions are much more sophisticated and subtle today. Our Lord warned, *"For false Christs and false prophets shall rise, and shall shew signs and wonders, to seduce, if it were possible, even the elect"* (Mark 13:22).

I am thankful for all the labor of TBC ministry through the years and the fruit that has come forth and blessed many. They have been a blessing to us. If we continue to stay the course that the Lord established at the beginning and hold to our convictions, fruit, more fruit—much fruit—will abound, and our Heavenly Father will be glorified. (John 15:8)

Paul urges us to consider two things that are of utmost importance. The first is *"Not that we are sufficient of ourselves to think anything as of ourselves; but our sufficiency is of God."* Whatever we are deficient in, He is sufficient. If we lack something, He is sufficient to provide what is necessary.

And the second thing to remember is that [He] *"also hath made us able [sufficient] ministers of the new testament; not of the letter, but of the Spirit: for the letter killeth, but the Spirit giveth life"* (2 Cor. 3:5-6).

Amazing as it is, He has given us (every believer) the capability to be New Testament ministers. Having been born again, we have received the Spirit of God, who dwells within us and enables us to understand His Word and obey it.

Not only that, but we can also minister His Word, building up one another in the faith. Our Lord, His Word, and the ministry of the Holy Spirit are sufficient to supply all our needs according to His riches in glory in Christ Jesus.

Conclusion

As I conclude, I would like to refer you to the passage that I shared near the beginning of this booklet. These two verses are profitable to meditate on and memorize. They are indeed life changing and applicable to many things we encounter throughout our life. Allow the Lord to give you thoughts you might not have considered up to this point.

> *"Remember ye not the former things, neither consider the things of old. Behold, I will do a new thing; now it shall spring forth; shall ye not know it? I will even make a way in the wilderness, and rivers in the desert." (Isa. 43:18-19)*

Even though the Lord has blessed in the past and done wonderful things for you, He is calling you and says, *"Behold, I will do a new thing."* He wants you to *"Behold."* However, if you are still dwelling on *"former things"* and *"things of old,"* how will you be able to *"behold"* the new thing that He is doing? With expectant eyes of faith, we are to look ahead, as He said, *"Now it shall spring forth."* He then asks the question, *"Shall ye not know it?"*

On the other hand, will you not be aware of it? He wants us to be cognizant of it. He wants us to recognize what He is doing. It will be something new that we will praise Him for because only *"He is able to do exceedingly abundantly above all that we ask or think, according to the power that worketh in us"* (Ephesians 3:20).

He will lead us out of the spiritually desolate wasteland where there was only stagnant murky water to drink (of which many have become accustomed) and, as He said, *"I will even make a way in the wilderness, and rivers in the desert"* (Isa. 43:18-19).

We must believe this and understand what John the Baptist said: *"A man can receive nothing, except it be given him from heaven"* (John 3:27).

We want to receive only what the Lord gives us from above and nothing else! We need the Lord to teach us New Testament reality and not merely settle for what we have known. I thought that the paradigm with which I had become familiar at my former church was a part of New Testament when in reality it was not. Ask God to quicken your understanding in the book of Acts and the epistles as to what is New Testament reality.

Let Him do a wondrous thing in your life and in the lives of those around you. That is what He does! As it says in Psalm 72:18: *"Blessed be the Lord God, the God of Israel, who only doeth wondrous things."*

Call out to Him and ask, as David did in Psalm 25:4-5: *"Show me thy ways, O Lord; teach me thy paths. Lead me in thy truth, and teach me: for thou art the God of my salvation; on thee do I wait all the day."*

Below is the Q and A that Dave Hunt responded to that blessed us significantly.

QUESTION:

We can't seem to find a church in our area that has godly leadership and biblical preaching. We feel so alone and now just read the Bible and pray at home. What should we do? How do we find a good church?

RESPONSE:

It is a sad commentary on the state of the church that we receive many such queries. What marks a "healthy" church? Crucial to the answer is Matthew 18:20: *"For where two or three are gathered together in my name, there am I in the midst. . . . "* Christ himself must be the central focus—not a pastor, gripping sermons, a strong missionary emphasis, exciting youth programs, compatible fellow members, or even agreeable doctrines, important as all these factors are. A fervent love for Christ and a heartfelt corporate worship of His Person must be the primary mark of a healthy church.

Priority One: Worship

The early church was thus characterized. It met regularly on the first day of the week in remembrance of His death. That weekly outpouring of praise, worship, and thanksgiving had one purpose—to give God His due portion. It isn't primarily a matter of my need, my edification, my enjoyment, or my spiritual satisfaction, but of His worth in my eyes and in the eyes of the church.

Secondary Focus: Servanthood

As I see it, our secondary focus should be our opportunity for servanthood with a corporate body of believers. I give myself to a needy, imperfect people for whom I can pray, with whose needs I can concern myself in practical ways, to whom I can be an encourager and a minister of the Word, and among whom I can demonstrate and work out Christ's desire that His own "might be one." This fellowship is commanded: "Not forsaking the assembling of ourselves together" (Heb. 10:25).

Is it our *joy* to gather with God's people in intercessory prayer and study of the Word—or is Sunday-morning-only quite enough? A healthy church will gather not only unto Him but *with* each other.

Personal Needs

Lastly, I need to assess my own spiritual needs. The shepherds must provide the *spiritual food* that will nurture the flock, that it might be "thoroughly furnished unto all good works" (2 Tim. 3:17). That's a big order and requires, of course, a teachable flock that loves the Word and is in willing subjection to it. The shepherds must also guard the flock of God *by keeping out false and dangerous doctrines* contrary to the truth. They must adhere to the pure Word of God as the only authority for faith and morals.

You say, "Wonderful! Lead me to such a church."

Remember, however, the order of priority: *worship* (do you worship sincerely, wholeheartedly, and in a manner satisfying to the Object of that worship?); *servanthood* (do you serve, even as Christ gave us an example, with humility and with joy?); *personal needs* (are you growing, maturing, taking on Christ's character?).

The final decision as to your church affiliation must be, prayerfully, yours. Is your personal worship of the Savior so joyful and satisfying a thing both to you and to Him that it supersedes other considerations?

Do your opportunities for service render your fellowship sufficiently meaningful and significant? Or do doctrinal concerns or lack of biblical preaching and teaching cancel out the other two?

You must seek the Lord for His answer. God's comforting assurance remains:

> *"For where two or three are gathered together in my name, there am I in the midst of them."*

THE AUTHORS

DAVE KERCHER has served on the board of directors for The Berean Call, since its beginning in 1992, being one of the founding board members. Dave has also served for many years on the Board of directors for Shield of Faith Mission International, which is a ministry that honors the scriptures as the word of God, and seeks to glorify the Lord Jesus, as does TBC.

Dave served as an elder in Bend Bible Fellowship, which meets in Bend, Oregon from 1989 to 1999, which was the home fellowship for Dave & Ruth Hunt. Dave has served as an elder for the last 18 years in Bible Family Fellowship, which meets in Molalla, Oregon. Both of these fellowships are committed to being true to the scriptures, in the liberty and function of the ministries of the church, as described in the booklet that Dave has authored.

PETE F. SALAS was born in Colorado. In 1975, as a musician, he moved to California and began traveling the country performing. In the summer of 1978, while still traveling, Pete came to faith in the Lord Jesus Christ in his hotel room. Within a few weeks, he left the music profession moving back to California. At the church he attended, he was part of a gospel group and participated in the church orchestra. However, his love for the Scriptures prompted him to go to Bible College. A bible teacher also trained him for a number of years. Pete began teaching Sunday school classes and weeknight Bible studies. He also taught the gospels in his home reaching the lost.

In 1991, Pete helped start a fellowship group that eventually became a home church where he was one of the overseers. In 1998, he and his family moved to Colorado. Pete has been a board member of The Berean Call since 2013. Throughout the years, he has continued to have home bible studies. He also disciples young men one on one in the Scriptures. Pete and his wife participate in a home assembly.